LISTEN TO MY

♥ HEART ♥

LISTEN TO MY ♥ HEART ♥

Lessons in Love, Laughter, and Lunacy

Kathie Lee and Cody Gifford

ILLUSTRATIONS BY SANDRA FORREST

HYPERION

NEW YORK

Library of Congress Cataloging-In-Publication Data:

Gifford, Kathie Lee, 1953–
    Listen to my heart: lessons in love, laughter, and lunacy/Kathie Lee and Cody Gifford: illustrations by Sandra Forrest.—1st ed.
        p.   cm.
    ISBN 0-7868-6075-8
    1. Mother and child—United States—Anecdotes. 2. Mothers—United States—Anecdotes. 3. Women television personalities—United States—Family relationships. 4. Gifford, Kathie Lee, 1953—. I. title
HQ755.85.G54   1995
306.874'3—dc20   94–38453
                                                                    CIP

DESIGNED BY JESSICA SHATAN

FIRST EDITION

10 9 8 7 6 5 4 3 2 1

For all the innocent children who
come into this world
without love and without hope.

FOREWORD

This is a book that any mother and her child could have written. Many do write down the wonderful moments, the special conversations, and the hysterical episodes that happen in their lives.

But these stories are uniquely Cody's and mine. I treasure every one, and I could have locked them away privately like most mothers do, except for one thing: By sharing them with you, many children who will never know such moments will have their lives touched, made more comfortable, and in some cases even be saved.

I don't know why I feel such a responsibility for these children who are so different from my own. But I always have. And now Frank does. And Cody. And someday soon I know Cassidy will, too.

No, they aren't my children, or yours—but they are precious, and God has asked us to make them ours.

Cody and I are honored to dedicate this book to these children, whom we know only by their first names. And more important, we dedicate our lives to making theirs better.

LISTEN TO MY
♥ HEART ♥

SOMETIMES I LOOK AT MY KIDS PLAYING TOGETHER and laughing and tackling and kissing each other and I'm tempted for just a moment to think that all is well in the world. Then out of the blue Cassidy will fall and hit her head, and I'll get angry at Cody for being too rough. And then I'm reminded that life is all too fragile. It can all change in just an instant. And just realizing that is so frightening to me as a parent.

I think we spend all our time trying to make the world as perfect and as comfortable and as happy as possible. And then spend the rest of our time trying to keep at bay the things that would change any of that. And it's exhausting. Just the worrying is exhausting. You want to let them grow and run and experience the grass under their toes, but at the same time, you're wondering if there's a snake in the grass or a sharp object or a stone. Anything that's gonna hurt them.

The challenge of being a parent is finding the right balance between letting them go and hanging on to them for dear life. I'm finding it a little different with Cassidy than with Cody. I'm finding I'm less frightened for her, even though she's a girl. I guess because Cody was my first and everything was new. Now I realize that you do survive the scrapes and the bee stings and falling out of bed and all the things that you're so terrified of with your first child. You realize that there's life after these things. And so you tend to just relax a little bit, I guess, with the second one.

She's such a tough little thing. But to see those crocodile tears streaming down her face is just…you wonder if there's anything more terrifying or more beautiful at the same time as your child lifting up her face to you with the tears streaming down with the look of, number one, how did that happen and, number two, what are you going to do about it, Mom? Some days, I just feel so capable of doing it all. Just dealing with every crisis, dealing with every moment, dealing with their little scuffles and their needs. And other days I just feel so overwhelmed by it, and so inadequate. ❧

TODAY WAS CODY'S FIRST DAY OF SCHOOL. AND I'M driving now in the car to pick him up and meet his teacher and take him to lunch to celebrate. And I'm kind of embarrassed by the fact that I was far more nervous than he was. He was all gung ho and couldn't wait to get back to the classroom. And he said, "I'm going to be in a different, bigger class-room this year. I'm going to have a differ-ent teacher." All the things I thought he would be frightened by are the things that he was excited about. So you think you know your kid, and you find out that your kid is way ahead of you.

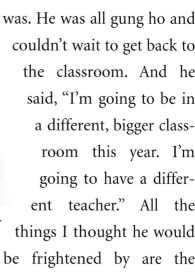

It makes me happy to know that he's not frightened of the new things in life but is sort of embracing them and looking forward to them. That's what my folks did for me, when I think back on it. They created in me such a sense of well-being and security that the next day was always an adventure. I don't remember being very frightened about anything.

I guess that's your job as a parent: to make your children aware of the things that are healthy to be frightened of and create a sense of excitement in them about the things that they should be excited about and not fearful of, like the first day of school, like going to the doctor and the dentist. So, so far so good. But the day is young. ❧

WHEN CODY FIRST STARTED SCHOOL I STARTED LEAVING notes for him in the morning before I left for work. The only bad thing about my job is that I do leave before he's awake, and I miss that really sweet time when there are Cheerios all over the place and spilled milk and *Good Morning America* on the TV. Just sort of the coziness of that. And I get up and basically throw my clothes on and get in the car and go and read the papers and have a cup of coffee and a Slim Fast bar in the car. So I really do cherish the times when we can have breakfast.

I started leaving little notes a couple of years ago for Cody, just to let him know I'm aware that I'm not having breakfast with him, aware that there's something that we're both missing. And helping him to be aware that he's really, really important to me and that I want his day to go well and that no matter what my schedule is, he—and now Cassidy, too—are always at the forefront of my mind. I would hate for them to think at any moment that something's more important than they are. There might be something more urgent at the moment that I have to take care of. But more important, no.

That's my real challenge right now. When the phone rings and they want me for whatever reason, it's a balancing act to sort of graciously let the person on the other end of the phone know that they're important, too, but not as important as my children.

Just yesterday I had to make a decision between a friend and my child. A friend's book was coming out and there was a book party for her. I had told her that if I possibly could, I'd be there. Which meant staying in the city all day long, going by her book party for fifteen minutes, just to wish her well, then fighting the rush hour traffic back to Connecticut so that I would at least be there to kiss Cassidy good night and get Cody in the bathtub and say his prayers and talk about the next day.

Well, the next day happened to be the first day of school. It was four o'clock, and as I waited in my apartment for six-thirty to arrive so I could go to the book party I just thought, you know, this is one of those times when I have to make a tough decision. It doesn't mean I don't care about my friend. But if she's a real friend she'll understand that Cody's got school the next day and that my place is with him. It's one of those times when you wish you could be two people at once. Be there for everybody. I always feel like I'm letting somebody down, no matter what I do. Even with the best intentions somebody's always gonna be on the short end of the stick, I guess. ❧

I'M IN CONSTANT AMAZEMENT OF THE LITTLE PEOPLE that are developing before my eyes. Cody is becoming such a little performer. And that doesn't frighten me. It really thrills me, frankly. Because being a performer has been one of the great joys of my life. Being a celebrity basically stinks. But being a performer and making your living at something you love to do is something that I've always been very grateful for.

He doesn't seem to be too interested in sports, except for your typical kid stuff. When there's a ball around he'll kick it, and if there's a bat he'll hit a ball a couple of times. Or if there's a swimming pool, he does love that. He'll stay in all day long—jumping out about a thousand times during the day. "Mommy,

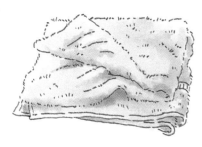

I'm chilly, I'm chilly, I'm chilly." He'll want some big towel to be wrapped around him, and he'll sit in the sun on top of me or on top of Christine and just get held and warm, and

then he'll jump back in. And he's got the whitest head of hair this year. He's mister chlorine.

So he's athletic in that sense, but I don't think he's ever going to have the drive or the passion for sports the way his dad did. And that's just fine with both of us. But he does love to perform. It's amazing how he can now mimic any movie he's watched or song he's heard. And he loves that commercial, "Pardon me, have you any Grey Poupon?" So he kept saying that to me with his French accent. One day I just responded to him in my own French accent. "Have I any Grey Poupon? Monsieur, I *am* Grey Poupon. I poop on this, I poop on that, I poop on everything."

Well, of course his bathroom humor is absolutely his favorite thing in the world. And that took off like crazy in our family. It's been "Grey Poupon" around our house for about a week now. Anybody who will listen, he'll do it for them about five, six times.

As much as you can take, he'll deliver it. And maybe somebody would be aghast that I would say such a thing as "I poop on this, I poop on that." But to me that is such a harmless sort of fun thing to do, to make light of a perfectly human activity.

I want him to feel healthy about things like that. I want him to feel healthy about his body. I like to let him run around as he calls out, "I'm nudist, I'm nudist." Running around the house and running outside in the yard and swimming naked—I love the innocence of all that. I mean, soon enough the world will let him know that there's a prurient side to being naked. But for right now I think it's good that he knows his body is a healthy thing. And a gift.

And eventually I want him to understand that it's the temple of God, and that he is a creature of God's creativity. And I want him to be very healthy, ultimately, with his sexuality. I don't want him to be gross, but I think it's kind of cute that he knows he's a boy, he knows he's different, he knows that Daddy and he are able to go potty in the bush and we have to go into the house, a long ways away. Sometimes I say, "Frank, please take him into the bathroom like a normal human being!" And then I wonder, how normal do I want him to be? Right now he's interesting and fascinating to me. And I'm just so over-whelmed with him. Just a sense of gratitude that he's so unique and so very precious. ❧

NEVER KNOW HOW MUCH TO SHARE ABOUT MY CHIL-
dren. I'm just a normal mom who's really proud of them, and I
would love to just go on and on and on about them. I guess
some people have accused me of that. But the truth is that I
really choose which stories I'll tell very carefully now. I'm very
aware of the repercussions of what I say. I don't want to see some
really precious story that's been turned around to be something
bizarre end up on the cover of tabloids.

For every sweet thing in life there's somebody who wants to
come along and spoil it. I'm frightened these days that anything
I might say or do would be harmful to my kids, ultimately. I'm
more sure than ever, and so is Frank, that we will sue to our last
day anybody who lies about our children or hurts them in any
way. And we'll spend the rest of our days in court if we have to.

Then I say to myself, oh, why even mention them? Why say
one word and even give anybody a chance to be cruel to them in

any way? And then I get letters from lovely people all over the country who love hearing the stories about Cody and miss knowing what's going on in Cassidy's life.

It's not that I feel obligated, it's just that I know there are sweet, wonderful people out there because I hear from them in my own mail. And I meet them in airports and at our concerts and appearances. And I can just see the goodness on their faces. I would love to be able to share with them all the little things that friends share with one another, and I'm sad that I don't have the freedom to do that. ❧

IN THE SUMMER OF 1993, WE had just moved into a new house in Colorado. We had just had Cassidy, so it was a very exciting time in our life. I think Cassidy was about twelve days old when we flew out to Colorado and spent the first night in our new house. We were just thrilled. And President Ford and Betty Ford lived half the year out in Beaver Creek, Colorado. They're just two of the dearest, dearest people I've ever known. I've always felt so privileged to not only know a former president and his wife, but to know them as people. It is a really special thing in Frank's and my life.

And when we first got out to Colorado last summer, we called them and asked them to please be our very first guests for dinner in our new home. Betty called and said, "Hi, Kathie, it's Betty." And I had to remind myself, my gosh, that's Betty Ford.

So I invited them for dinner. And she said, no, no, no, you just had the new baby, you just moved into a new house, the last thing in the world you need is dinner guests. But we will come by and see the kids, and then why don't we just all go to dinner real close by. So I said, well, that's a great compromise and that will work out fine.

In the meantime, I'd been waiting for our new sofas to arrive. I'd been promised, pretty much every day—there was a new update every day—our sofas were coming, our sofas were coming. They'd been ordered from North Carolina, and I was assured that they were on their way. Well, they never came. I was getting more and more frustrated.

Finally, on the morning of the day that the President and Mrs. Ford were due to arrive at our house at six o'clock, I got a call that my sofas were, indeed, on their way. They were just outside of Denver. They would be there by three o'clock that afternoon, absolutely for sure. Well, I was thrilled. I thought, Three o'clock, that gives me time to move the ugly old sofas we have in the living room all the way up to Cody's playroom, sixty feet up in our loft. And we'd have the nice open spaces right there ready for the sofas for the President and Mrs. Ford to sit on when they came over at six.

Well, needless to say, by three o'clock the sofas were nowhere to be seen; by four o'clock, nowhere to be seen. Now I'm looking at two gaping holes in my living room. Now the sofas that are up there in Cody's playroom are looking beautiful and I'm wondering, Why the heck did I ever move those? Those weren't so bad. They were beautiful sofas. And I'm thinking, we've still got time.

Well, the Secret Service arrived around five o'clock to check out the property. And all of a sudden this huge wind came up. Now I'm saying, My gosh, when are these sofas gonna get here? And Frank's gonna kill me if the sofas aren't here. . . . Now I'm getting an update from the Secret Service that the President and Mrs. Ford are on their way up the mountain. We live eight thousand feet up on a very, very windy mountainous road.

Also, I have heard from the sofa people out in Avon, Colorado, that they have indeed seen the truck with the sofas on it and they are on their way. I'm thinking, Oh my gosh, if only the sofas would make it before the President and Mrs. Ford. Well, it was a fiasco. It was a comedy of errors. It was just like an old episode of *I Love Lucy* with Ricky looking at Lucy and going, "Aiee, Lucy, I'm going to kill you." Those were the looks Frank was giving me. He never wanted me to move the sofas to begin with. He never wanted me to order new sofas to begin with. In fact, he never wanted more children.

And now we've got the President and Mrs. Ford coming and no sofas to sit on. Cassidy's crying in the background; she needs to be changed; she's a newborn. I was nursing her at the time. It was unbelievable.

So anyway, needless to say, the sofas do arrive. One guy gets out of this huge semi truck, an enormous wind is blowing, and Frank's outside talking to this guy, trying to bribe him to get the sofas into our living room before the President arrives. And this guy's looking at him like, sure, mister, sure the President's coming for dinner. And Frank keeps throwing looks at me in the kitchen like, I'm going to kill you, Kathie. Any minute now I'm going to kill you. I considered saving him the effort and doing it myself.

Well, the sofas were all crated and wrapped. It would have been impossible to get them into our living room in time to have the President and Mrs. Ford sit on them. So instead we decided to just throw them in the garage. Because, indeed, now

President and Mrs. Ford were at the front door. So, we just decided, they're the nicest people in the world; they will understand. They've had children of their own; they've ordered sofas before; they've moved into new houses, and they'll be great about it.

Well, here we are standing at our entranceway, which has a landing. You look down into our living room and then you look up into Cody's loft. And there, of course, are the sofas that I should have never moved. And there down below, of course, there's just a gaping hole looking at me. And I immediately explain to the President and Mrs. Ford why the sofas aren't there. And I apologize and they're as gracious as they possibly can be.

So I decide, well, at least I've got an adorable son. Now, what I forgot to tell you is that all week long I'd been training Cody to say, "Good evening, President Ford, good evening, Mrs. Ford." And he was great. Every time I asked him to do it he was absolutely perfect. Well, now we don't have the sofas so I'm thinking, I know what I can do, I can introduce them one more time to my adorable son. I said, "Cody, don't you have something to say to President and Mrs. Ford?" He looks at them, puts on his nasty face, says, "Nothing," and runs away.

Well, now I'm thinking, Great, what can I do? I know, I'll put them in the one little room that we do have decorated adorably. It does actually have a little love seat, and I'll serve cocktails. And then I think to myself, You can't serve cocktails to the woman who started the Betty Ford Clinic, for goodness sake.

So I think, Well, I'll serve them hors d'oeuvres. So I sit them down and get them a tonic water. We're sitting there chatting and all of a sudden Cody comes in and he's decided he's going to be charming, which is fine with me. He lies there next to us, and we're having a lovely conversation. Although Frank is still not really thrilled with me.

All of a sudden I smell something a little funny. And I start to sniff. Now, Cody's supposed to be potty trained. And I said, "Cody, is there something in your pants?" And he looks up and with a very loud voice says, "No, I'm just tooting." Well, now I'm dying. I said, "Cody, you get out of here, get out of here this instant." So he scoots off.

I'm just starting to get everything under control and calm, and everybody's having a lovely time when I hear Cody scream from the other room, "Somebody come and wipe my buns, somebody come and wipe my buns!" I'm mortified. I run out. He's in the bathroom. He's got poo all over him. He's got diarrhea. I said, "Oh, Cody, I can't believe this." I'm so upset, so frustrated by now. No sofas, can't serve cocktails, no adorable child. Just the President, that's all . . . . all I've got is the President and his wife sitting in my cowboy room.

And I just decide that's it. I just go back into the room and join them when all of a sudden Cody comes in with his pants down and announces to the President and Mrs. Ford, "I've got diarrhea!" Well, that's it. At that point I just decide to end it all. Mrs. Ford was so adorable. She started laughing and said, "Oh, sweetheart, we've got grandchildren of our own, you know." And I just thought, Maybe that's why I like these people so much. They're so real. And so's my kid. ❧

CODY WAS HAVING TROUBLE WITH HIS MANNERS. He didn't understand why his daddy and I (mostly I) thought they were so important. One day at the dinner table he refused to put his napkin on his lap.

"Cody," I scolded, "I've told you over and over to put your napkin on your lap. Now, there will be no treat after supper unless you put it back and LEAVE IT THERE."

"Mom, do pirates put their napkins on their laps?" he questioned.

"No, Cody," I said, "pirates are the worst; they have no manners at all."

At this Cody got excited. "What do they do?" He laughed,

thinking there must be nothing better in the world than being a pirate.

"Well," I said very seriously, "for one thing, they never take a bath."

"Never?" he yelled. "Not even a shower?"

"Never," I said, "so they smell very stinky."

"Cool!" Cody smiled.

"And they always talk with their mouths full, and all the food slobbers all over their faces and drips down their chins and falls on their laps 'cause they don't use any napkins."

Now Cody was practically screaming, "And what else do pirates do?"

"Well"—I was starting to get a little caught up in this myself—"they never share, and they never brush their teeth, and they never say 'please' or 'thank you.' "

"Yes!" Cody shrieked. "What else?"

"They burp and they toot and they bite their nails, and they never wash their hands after they go potty." By now I was exhausted from trying to think of disgusting things that pirates do.

"Mom," Cody said as he thought this over, "do pirates eat their boogs?"

"*Yes!*" I yelled, happy to have some help. "That's the thing that is the *most disgusting* of all!"

Now Cody was *sure* he wanted to be a pirate.

ONE DAY I TAUGHT CODY HIS FIRST JOKE. "CODY,"
I asked, "how do you make your handkerchief dance?"

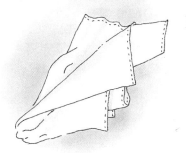

"I know," he laughed. "You put a
little boogie in it!"

LATELY CODY HAS TAKEN TO MIMICKING EVERYTHING he hears and sees. And I never know when it's going to come out. The other day we were sitting at the dinner table, and he said, "Mom, I've got a problem."

I said, "What is it, Cody?"

He answered, "Mom, are we broke?"

Well, needless to say, where in the world did he hear that? I'm thinking, What did somebody tell him? We just moved and so we can't afford a curtain or a . . . I mean, what's going on? And he said, "Blank check, Mom." Well, darn if he wasn't right. We'd just been watching a movie called *Blank Check,* and he mimicked the movie perfectly. (Remind me not to let him see *Last Tango in Paris!*) ❧

LATELY HONESTY'S BEEN A BIG DEAL AT OUR HOUSE. I've really been trying to teach Cody how important it is to be honest—honest with your feelings, honest in your dealings with people. And maybe I've been hitting it home too hard because the other day my friend Eva, his godmother, showed up with all kinds of Power Rangers toys, which I've asked her not to bring. And all kinds of Power Rangers candy, which I'd asked her not to bring. But nothing stops Eva. And she is, after all, his godmother.

So, anyway, I told Cody he could not have the Power Rangers sucker. He just couldn't have it. And he said okay. So he put it away and about an hour later he came to me and said, "Mom, can I have the sucker if I promise not to lick it?" I thought, All right.

Sure, I'll give him a chance. I'll trust you with this, Cody. I said, "You may play with it. But you may not lick it." He said okay.

About half an hour later, I was playing tennis and he came up and said, "See, Mom, I didn't lick it." And I said, "Cody, I'm very proud of you. I trusted you and you did right." Then he added, "But, Mom, I did smell it." And I answered, "Well, that's okay, Cody. That wasn't part of the deal."

He said, "But, Mom, you know when I was smelling it?" And I said, "Yeah." He said, "Well, I rubbed it under my nose so I could smell it really, really good."

I asked, "You mean really well?"

He replied, "Yeah, so I could smell it really well." And I said, "Yeah." And he said, "Well, it got on my nose." And I said, "Well, that's okay."

But then, "Mom, you know how I can touch my tongue to my nose?" And I said, "Yeah."

"Well, then I licked my nose with my tongue."

And I said, "Cody, I'm very, very proud of you. You told me the truth."

He seemed very pleased with this. And I said, "Cody, because you told me the truth I want to reward you." And so I gave him the sucker.

What are you gonna do? ❧

CODY WAS A REAL STAY-AT-HOME KIND OF GUY, always preferring to play at home than go just about anywhere. (Except Disney World. He'd go to Disney World *anytime.*) So I was worried about telling him that we would soon be moving to a new house. "Cody," I asked one day, trying to sound casual, "wouldn't it be cool to move to a *new* house and sleep in a *new* bed and make new friends in a *new* neighborhood?"

Cody wasn't sure this sounded so great. "Where will you live, Mom?" he asked me.

"With you, you silly goose!" I reassured him. I picked him up and held him tight.

"Cool!" he cried. "Mom, *you're* my home."

"MOM, I'M GONNA BE BIG," CODY ANNOUNCED one day to me.

"How big, Cody?" I asked.

"As big as I wanna be," he answered. He strutted around the kitchen like he was big stuff already.

"How big do you want to be?" I asked him.

At this, Cody stretched up on his toes and reached as high as he could. "Fifty feet high!" he said.

"Cody," I laughed, "That's eight daddies!"

This news pleased him a lot.

"That's big enough," he said, and ran off to save the world. ☙

ONE NIGHT, I ASKED
Cody what he thought
was important in this
world.

"You mean like
toys and stuff?" he asked,
lining up his dinosaurs for
a final battle before I put
him to bed.

"No, honey," I said, "like
family and friends and stuff like
that."

"Oh, like Grandma and Pop-pop
and Chrissie?"

"That's right. You know what I think is the
most important thing in the whole wide world?"

"What?" he asked, finally putting away his tyrannosaurus rex and his triceratops.

"Love," I said. "I think love is the most important thing in the whole world."

"Nah." Cody shook his head.

"What's more important than love, Cody?" I asked.

At this, Cody's eyes got big as saucers. "Pots and pans!" he yelled.

"Pots and pans?" I asked.

"Pots and pans! Pots and pans!" he yelled, hysterical with laughter.

"Well," I said, "you do need pots and pans to cook your food and you do need food to stay alive, so…"

"See, Mom?" he howled.

O N A VERY WET AND STORMY SPRING NIGHT, CODY and I sat on our favorite love seat in his room to read a book. We like this spot because usually there's just the two of us and we're both usually a little sleepy by this time of day, and it's great to be together. Cody likes to hear the funny stories I tell him, and I enjoy adding all kinds of silly voices and even changing the stories sometimes.

After my story, we sat on the love seat and watched the spring

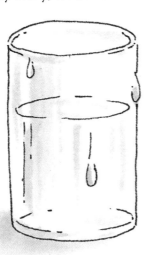

rain fall. I told Cody how important rain is, even though it sometimes spoils a picnic or a bicycle ride or a day at the beach. "Cody, without a drink of water, all God's creatures would die, including you and me. You know how you always want 'just a little bit' of a drink before you go to bed, and I always say 'just two sips'?"

"Or else I'll go peepee during the night!" Cody yelled out.

"That's right," I said. "Well, the earth is getting ready to go night-night, and it's asking God for 'just a little bit' before it goes to sleep, too."

Cody looked at all the water that was falling outside, all the puddles and little streams. "Well, that's a lot more than two sips," he said.

"Yeah, the earth's a little bigger than you are," I said.

Suddenly a huge clap of thunder rattled the window, and Cody's eyes became huge. He asked, "What's that?"

"That's God up in heaven with his angels," I replied.

Cody thought about this for a minute until an even bigger thunderbolt almost knocked him off his seat.

"No, Mama," he said, "God's in an airplane!"

I laughed. "Okay, big guy, time for night-night."

"Mama, can I have some water before I go to bed—just a little bit?"

"Okay, Cody, you little con artist," I laughed. "Just two sips." ꞊

ODY ISN'T ALWAYS A GOOD BOY, BUT HE WANTS TO be. One day he asked me, "Am I as bad as Dennis the Menace, or am I perfect?"

"Well, Cody," I laughed. "You're certainly not as bad as Dennis the Menace, but you're certainly not perfect either."

Now, Cody figured out that he must be something in between, and he wasn't sure that was good.

"So what am I?" he asked. He looked up at me with his gray-blue eyes. They usually twinkled with mischief or joy, but today I missed that twinkle.

"You're just perfect for me," I said, and gathered his gangly four-year-old arms and legs up in my arms as well as I could.

ONE REALLY HOT DAY IN JUNE, CODY AND I DECIDED to cool off together by going swimming. After lots of back flips, cannonballs, and races to the deep end, I asked if he wanted to play Marco Polo.

"What's that?" Cody asked.

"No, *who's* that," I said. "Marco Polo was a man who lived hundreds of years ago in a country called Italy." (Actually, I wasn't entirely sure about this, and I reminded myself to check my historical facts later.)

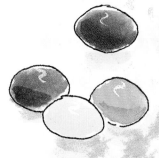

"What did he do?" Cody asked as he tried to put his goggles on.

"Well," I explained, "he was a famous explorer who traveled the world looking for wonderful things to bring back to his country."

"For show-and-tell!" Cody shrieked.

"Well, sort of," I laughed. "Actually, he became famous for traveling all the way to the Orient and bringing back all kinds of fabulous treats."

"Like Skittles!" Cody cried out. ❧

Back before Cassidy was born, I was excited and worried at the same time. I had big news for Cody, and hoped he would be as happy about it as I was. Bedtime was usually the best time for serious talk, so I waited until we cuddled on the love seat after reading some books.

"Cody," I began, snuggling him close to me, "how would you like to have a little brother or sister?"

"Yes!" Cody screamed, making karate chops in the air. "Then I would have a friend to play with!"

"That's right," I said. I was relieved that he seemed so excited.

"But, Mom," he continued, suddenly more serious, "I want a baby sister."

I smiled. "Well, I don't want you to be disappointed. You know it might be a brother or a sister."

"It's a baby sister, Mom." At this he smiled wisely.

We sat there thinking for a while, when suddenly he asked, "Mom, will you be my baby sister's mother, too?"

"Yes," I answered. "But who will be my mother?" he asked.

"I will, you silly goose," I said.

"That's okay, Mom." Cody patted me. "I'll get another Mommy."

I wasn't sure I was too happy with his news. ꙮ

CODY SAT IN HIS BATHTUB ONE NIGHT, MAKING
sure it was just as wet outside as inside.
(This made me crazy.)
After I warned him
one more time what
would happen if he got
another drop on the floor, Cody suddenly said,
"Mom, heaven is full of old people, right?"

I was surprised by his question, but I was busy mopping up the mess on the floor.

"That's right, Cody," I said pretty firmly, because I was still a little upset with him.

"Old people like *you*," he said.

"MOM, WHERE DO BABIES COME FROM?"

Cody and I were lying in Noah's Ark one night. It was getting pretty tight in the ark because I was getting really big in the stomach. Cody loved to put his hand on my tummy and feel the baby moving. "Mom, she's a wild woman!" he'd say as he felt a fist or a hand or a big kick. "She's crazy!"

"I know," I laughed, trying to get into a comfortable position. "I think she's just real anxious to come out and play with you."

In a moment, after we both settled down, I couldn't help saying, "Cody, where do you think babies come from?"

Cody thought about this for a moment and said, "I think they come from God. I think God grows them in his garden."

I smiled. "I think you're right, Cody."

"Mommy? When Cassidy comes, I will pwo-tect her."

"I know you will. You'll be the best brother in the world."

"Yeah." ❧

I WAS CONVINCED ONE DAY THAT CODY was being a little too rough with his baby sister.

"Cody," I warned him, "you have to be careful with Cassidy."

"Why?" he asked. "Because she's fragile?"

"That's right," I said, proud that he used such a big word and used it in the right way.

"What does *fragile* mean, Cody?" I asked to make sure he understood.

Cody looked up with a serious face and said, "It means she could break."

I gave him a big hug. "Cody, you're so smart."

I watched my two children playing on the floor. Every minute or so, Cody would put down whatever sword or Power Ranger

he was playing with and pull Cassidy toward him, kissing her over and over on the top of her head. "Careful, Cody, remember you said she was fragile," I warned.

"I know, Mom," Cody said, kissing her again, "but why do I love her little head so much?"

"I don't know," I laughed. "Why do you think?"

"Because it's so sweet," he answered, kissing her again. Cassidy started to wiggle away.

"Cody, do you remember when you were little and we kissed you all the time and you would say 'too many kisses'?"

"Yeah, but do you know what, Mom?"

"What?" I asked.

"You can never have too many kisses!"

CODY WAS ONLY THREE AND A HALF WHEN THE BATtle began. "Mom, can I watch *Power Rangers*?"

"What's *Power Rangers*, Cody?"

"It's really cool and it's on Fox Television."

"I've never heard of it, Cody," I answered. "Let Mommy and Chrissie watch it first, and then we'll see if you can watch it."

"But I already watched it!" he exclaimed, suddenly saying, "Go, go Power Rangers!"

This surprised me. "Where did you watch it?" I asked. "Did you see a video?"

"No, I watched it with Rory and Michael when Daddy took me up to Boston," he said matter-of-factly. "Roy and Michael got to watch it."

"Well," I said, wiping milk off his chin, "Rory and Michael are older than you are, and I'm not sure you're old enough yet to watch."

"Why?" he asked. "Because it's too *violent*?"

"Yes, honey. I don't want you to think that fighting is a good thing."

"But the Power Rangers are the good guys!" he argued. "They fight the bad guys and they *always win*! I'm going to be a Power Ranger when I grow up!" Now Cody started mimicking the Power Rangers, kicking in the air and grunting and yelling, "Zordon, we need Dinosaur Power—now!"

At this I said, "Well, Cody, I'm glad you want to grow up and be a good guy, but I'm still going to watch it first."

"Aw, Mom, *please,* I've just gotta watch *Power Rangers!* It's important!"

"Why, Cody?"

" 'Cause that's where I'll learn my *martial arts.*"

For weeks we argued about watching *Power Rangers*. Then one day we made a deal. I watched it with him. "Cody," I said when it was over, "that's the silliest show I've ever seen."

"I know, Mom," he said laughing. "I told you it's not violent. It's *hysterical.*"

Now we both love *Power Rangers.* ❧

ONE SPRING NIGHT CODY WAS CLIMBING INTO Noah's Ark when he asked me a very serious question. "Mom, does everybody have to die?"

"Well," I stuttered, surprised at his question, "yes, Cody, but it's not a scary thing."

"It isn't?"

"No, honey, it's just as natural to die as it is to be born. Remember last fall, when all the leaves fell off the trees and the trees looked so naked and lonely and sad, and you asked me why all the leaves had to die?"

"Uh-huh."

"And remember I told you, 'Just wait, when spring comes the trees will be prettier than ever—they'll get brand new leaves and grow bigger and taller?"

"Yes."

"Well," I continued, "that's sort of the way it is with us when we die as long as we have God in our hearts."

"Why?"

"Well, sweetheart, if we have God in our hearts when we die, we go to a wonderful place called heaven that is so much better than here on earth."

"How is it better?" he asked.

"It's better because in heaven there is no sickness and no sadness and no one goes hungry and no one is lonely. There's nothing in heaven but love."

"Do I have to go to bed early?" he asked.

"No, darling." I smiled. "You don't have to go to bed early."

"Goodie!" he yelled, finally climbing under the covers, "I can watch *Power Rangers*!" ❧

"CODY, WE NEED TO PRAY FOR SOME PEOPLE VERY far away." We were snuggled in the ark saying our usual good-night prayers.

"Who are they, Mommy?" he asked me, turning his pillow over to the "chilly side."

"Well, honey," I answered, "they live in a country called Rwanda and that's in Africa—you know, where the Lion King lives—and many of the people are dying there."

"Why, Mommy? What happened to them?"

Now Cody's voice was filled with concern. I wanted to answer him honestly, but I didn't want to make him afraid or burden a little boy with big-people problems. "Cody, in Rwanda, they had a war. Some bad men, just like Scar, wanted all the power, so they took that power by hurting the innocent people. Then the people got frightened and decided to go to another country to be safe. But when they got to the new country they drank water that wasn't clean, and they got sick from the water."

I sighed with sadness. "Now many more people are dying because they're sick and they don't have any food or clean water, and they need help."

"Mommy, I will share my grilled cheese with them!" At this Cody got excited. "We can send them our food, Mommy, and some toys, too!"

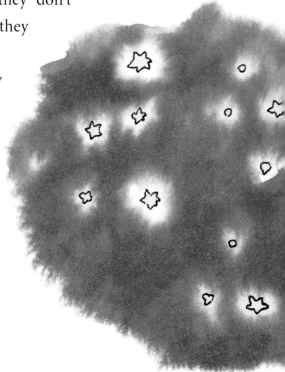

I smiled. "Cody, I love you for that. We'll send them some money to buy food. Okay? But for right now the best thing we can do is to pray for them every day until they get better, okay?"

"Okay, Mommy," Cody answered as he took one leg out from under the covers. "But I'm still gonna share my grilled cheese."

"I love you, Cody." I smiled as we both drifted off to sleep. ❧

ONE BEAUTIFUL SUNDAY MORNING CODY, FRANK, and I went to church. We hadn't been for a while, and we felt kind of bad about it. Most Sundays Cody put up a fuss if he had to go to Sunday school.

"No, Mommy! I want to stay at *my* house and play," he would say.

"We don't play on Sunday mornings, Cody," I would say to him again and again. "On Sundays we go to God's house and learn about Him."

Cody thought about this for a second. "Well, I can learn about Him at *MY HOUSE!*"

This particular Sunday, Cody didn't put up too much of a fight as he settled in between Frank and me in our little country church. Cody liked the singing part because everybody stood up and he got to stand on the pew to be as tall as Frank. He thought some of the people sang funny, though.

After a while a man came down the aisle carrying a plate, and

Cody watched as people passed the plate from one to another. "Mommy," Cody asked, tugging on my arm, "why are people putting money in that plate?"

"Well, honey," I answered (trying to be quiet because a lady was singing a really pretty song), "that's money people are sharing because God has blessed them and they want to show him how grateful they are. Do you want to put some money in it, too?" Cody got excited about this and stretched out his hand to take the three one-dollar bills I got out of my purse.

Suddenly he got an idea.

"Mommy!" he whispered conspiratorially, pulling my ear to his mouth. He held two bills in his left hand and one bill in his right hand. "I'll put these two in the plate—and I'll buy a toy with *this* one! Isn't that a great idea? Then God will see I'm *really grateful*!" ❧

"MOMMY, CAN I GET INTO BED WITH YOU?"

It was 5 A.M. and Frank and I were really sleepy. "Yes, Cody," I answered. "Climb on up."

"Good!" cried Cody, pulling himself onto the bed. "See, Mom, I brought my pillow *just in case!*"

I thought I had never loved him more as he snuggled close beside me and warmed his chilly feet against my warm ones.

"Good morning, sweetheart," I said to Frank. "We have company."

"Hi, Codes," Frank said, finally waking up. Cody didn't answer.

He was the only one asleep. ❧

NOBODY KNOWS HOW IT REALLY HAPPENED, BUT suddenly Cody and I became roommates one Sunday night during football season while his dad was away. Cody liked being the man of his house. He felt very protective of both me and his sister.

One Sunday night while cuddling and giggling, Cody suddenly asked, "Mommy, how old are you?"

I answered, "I'm forty-one."

Silence.

"When will you be twenty?"

I laughed. "Oh, honey, I *was* twenty, twenty-one years ago."

Silence.

"When will you be eight?"

I laughed again. "You're only eight once, Cody. I was eight a long time ago."

Silence.

"Mommy, when will you be a zillion?

"Oh, honey, nobody lives to a zillion."

"Daddy's a zillion!" Cody answered.

Silence. ❧

Once, during a particularly busy time in my life, when I didn't seem to have time to do anything, not even call my mother back on the phone, I was trying to get Cody to bed at night, and it was one of those kinds of evenings that he wanted to read a certain book. And the book he wanted to read was one that made me cry every time I read it. And so I said, "Cody, I'll read any other book you want, but I'm tired, I'm very emotional right now, and I don't trust myself to read that book to you."

He insisted, even though I read every other book he dragged off his bookcase. So...sure enough, I read *The Small One* to him. Which is, of course, the story of a little boy and his donkey, and how the father made the little boy go and sell his donkey because he had become too old to carry firewood anymore. So the little boy says, "Well, Daddy, then let me take him to sell him," to make sure he gets a good home. So he takes him to the marketplace, knowing he has to come home with one piece of silver. First the tanner wants to buy the donkey, but of course the boy doesn't want his friend to end up being a piece of hide hanging on the shelf. Then the auctioneer is willing to auction the donkey, but he's cruel to the animal. So the little boy runs away with his pet, and ultimately the donkey decides that the only thing to do is walk himself to the tanning shop and sacrifice his life, literally, for this little boy so he won't get in trouble with his father. And the little boy says, "If it means I never have to go home again, I will not do that to you." So they're just sitting there on the steps, when a man looks down on them and says, "Little boy, I've been spending all day long looking for a donkey to buy. I have only one piece of silver, but I promise I'll be good to your donkey and give him a good home." And wouldn't you know it, the end result of the story is that the little donkey ends up being the one that Joseph puts Mary on to ride all the way to Bethlehem, where she gives birth to baby Jesus.

Well, please—I was a disaster. I was an emotional wreck. Right at the part where the donkey decides to walk himself to the tanner's shop, I lost it. And there were still four pages to go. Cody kept looking at me like, Mom, get a grip. All right, Mom…Mom, it's just a story. But I'm losing it.

So anyway, I got through the story. I took him up to bed and tucked him in. We were saying our prayers, and he said, "Thank you God for Mommy and Daddy," and we went through the whole litany of people he has to pray for, and then he wanted to stop. "Mommy, let's just go night-night, now." And I said, "Cody, don't

One of my first concerns as a parent is how to teach my children about the dangers in the world without creating fear in them. In other words, getting them to be aware of the dangers in life without living a fearful life. I always notice that every fairy tale and every children's story seems to have a very evil person in it. Maybe some parents think that the best thing to do is not read them "Little Red Riding Hood" or "Snow White" or "The Three Little Pigs" or any of the stories that have a definite evil presence in them. But I always find that it gives me a chance to talk to my children about the scary things out there and what can hurt them. I try to use the opportunity to educate them and let us have quality time together.

One day Cody said, "Mommy, why is that guy mean?" referring to somebody in a story. I didn't want Cody to think that people are born mean. So I said, "Well, Cody, you know, maybe they never had a mommy and a daddy who loved them and taught them what was right in life. Maybe because they never had that love, they never learned how to love. It's not that they're so mean, it's just that they've never had any kindness in their life. So that's the only way they know to be. They've only known meanness, so they act mean."

He seemed to be pretty content with that answer. I didn't really think too much about it until one day when he was playing with his little friend, Robbie. And they were talking about some guy who had been mean to them. And I heard little Robbie say, "Why do you think he's so mean, Cody?" And I couldn't believe my ears when I heard Cody say, "Well, maybe he never had a mommy and a daddy who loved him." And it dawned on me that they hear *everything we say.* And they store it. And how important it is to say the right things to them and teach them the right way. Then I remembered that there's a scripture that says, Raise up a child in the way that they should go, and then when they are old, they will not depart from it.

That gave me great comfort, to know that I may be doing

some things wrong as a mother, but the one thing I *am* doing right is—while they are little—teaching them what is right. And they may go through their tough times as teenagers, or even young adults, but I have a promise I can count on and hold on to, and that is that when Cody and Cassidy are older, they will return to what is right because they were taught what was right when they were little. ❧

was on my way to an appoint-
ment when the phone call came
that Cody had fallen out of a tree.
Now, I know he's not supposed to be in
a tree—he was at school—but somehow
he'd fallen out. Frank went to get him at
the nurse's office, and I made the calls home, and he was fine. He
knows he shouldn't have been in the tree, and all is well, and no
real damage is done. But still, the question remains, for me—
would he have fallen out of the tree if I had been there? I mean,
even if I weren't a working mom, in the sense that I work outside
of the house, if I had been a stay-at-home mom and had sent my
kid to school, would it have happened? Obviously it would have
happened anyway; I can't stay with him at school the whole
time. But still, there are those lingering, nagging doubts I have
about not being there when he needs me. And I guess I'll have
them as long as I live. ❧

It's happening. I'm starting to sound like my mother. I guess it was inevitable. We are, after all, little computers, and whatever data's put in is what we become. I'm starting to hear myself say the same things to my children that my mother said to me: "Pick it up…clean up…use your napkin…you're gonna poke somebody's eye out with that thing…go to sleep…wait till your father comes home. . . . " All those things that are just so clichéd. But it happens.

I just hope that over the years my kids will feel the same way about me as I do about my mom. I was always the most important thing in the world to her.

Except twice. Twice, when I was a teenager, my mother was late getting home from shopping, having lunch with her friends, or whatever. And for some reason, we kids never had keys. So if anybody would ask me, "Was your mother the perfect mother?" I'd say yeah, except for those two times when I came home and I had to wait outside, having to go to the bathroom, while my mother took her own sweet time getting home from something. If that's all I can say, then she's done a pretty darn good job.

But remind me to give my kids their own keys.

One night we got home really late from a trip, so I decided to put both kids in the bath together to save time. Cody and Cassidy loved taking baths together, so for once nobody gave me a hard time.

Cody was being really sweet with his sister and sharing all his toys and saying things like, "Here you go, Precious. Here's a dinosaur for you."

After a while the bathtub was so filled with toys that there was hardly any room for the kids. All of a sudden, Cassidy tried to stand up to reach another toy. I said, "No, no, Cassidy, we sit down in the bathie." She knew by the serious tone in my voice that I meant it, so right away she sat her little buns down. But she sat down right on a stegosaurus! Now, if you know your dinosaurs, you know that the stegosaurus is not a good dinosaur to sit on because it has those sharp things on top.

Well, Cody just howled. Then Cassidy started to laugh. Pretty soon we were all just tickled crazy.

Then I said, "Cody, what else wouldn't be good to sit on?"

"A porcupine!" he yelled.

"A beehive!" I yelled back.

"An arrow!" Cody roared.

"An aardvark!" I screamed.

"I know something else that wouldn't be good to sit on," Cody said, laughing.

"What?" I asked.

"A lion!" he roared.

"You're right, Cody." I laughed with him. "That wouldn't be very good at all!"

Suddenly Cody got kind of quiet. "Mom, you know what else wouldn't be good to sit on?"

"What, Cody?"

"A flower."

"A flower?"

"Yeah." He laughed, covered with suds. "It wouldn't be good for the *flower!*" ❧

I've been thinking about the first time I realized that children are funny. I remember so clearly the first time I knew Cody was. I had to run and get a piece of paper and a pencil and write it down, because I didn't want to forget any of those special moments. In busy lives, it's so easy to just tell the story a few times and then keep going. But unless you write it down or record it or do something, it just gets lost. And that's a shame, because those stories really show their patterns of growth.

Cody was one of those babies that loved his binkie—his pacifier, of course. And he was very, very attached to this binkie. So attached that we worried how we were going to get the binkie out of his life. One day, we finally took the binkie from him. He looked everywhere for it. He said, "Mommy, what happened to my binkie?" I said, "Well, Cody, you didn't need it anymore, so we put it in the garbage. And the garbage man came, and he took it."

Well, after that, every time a garbage truck would go by, Cody would look at the truck, shake his fist, point, and say, "That guy took my binkie." I thought it was hysterical. And that's when I decided kids are funny. ❧

Recently I was taping a holiday family Christmas special. I had asked Cody, months before, if he wanted to be a part of it. I've never felt children should be forced to do something like that. It should be their choice, and then it should be made a fun learning experience for them.

Still, as we got closer to the taping date, I was very nervous. First of all, there was going to be a crew of forty people in our home, upsetting everything, bumping into things, making a mess. Then I wondered how Cassidy would deal with all of it. I thought of Frank, how he'd want to divorce me when he got off the road, came home, and found all these people in the house. And I wondered if Cody was going to be goofy when the time came to be serious and professional. Now, he's only four years old, so how professional can he be?

Buzz Kohan, the Emmy-winning writer on the special, had sent me a script a couple of weeks earlier for Cody to learn. I thought, he's so young; he can't learn a script. Well, he did learn it, and I was really, really proud. He did about five takes on each scene, and he was just excellent. I mean, I threw in a bribe here and there, definitely. But for a four-year-old, with that kind of concentration, not goofing up and not acting silly—I couldn't have been more proud.

Well, the taping went on for about a week. It was a nightmare, logistically and time-wise. I was just exhausted, worrying about my kids and my home and my husband. Plus I was still doing the show with Regis every morning.

One Sunday we went and taped for about four and a half hours at F.A.O. Schwarz. Earlier that day, Cody had packed up all his old toys and books. I have him do that every year before Christmas. We took them to the Cody House after we finished taping.

Because it was Sunday, there was only one little baby there. She was six months old, and her name was Samantha. But she was the size of maybe a two-month-old because of the crack addiction she was born into. She had a tube in her nose, and that's the way she was getting her milk.

Cody looked at her. He said, "Mommy, why is she getting her lunch that way?"

I said, "Well, Cody, when she was in her mommy's tummy, her mommy took some bad, bad things and didn't take care of herself, so she was born very, very sick."

Cody went over and took her tiny hand in his. He said, "Oh, Samantha, these toys will make you feel better." Which broke my heart.

Later that night, we were watching the Rolling Stones in an interview on *60 Minutes*. At one point they mentioned drugs. Cody looked at me and asked, "What are drugs?"

Of course, I wasn't planning on having this discussion with

Cody for a long, long time. But I said, "Well, Cody, you know how when you're sick I give you Tylenol, or the doctor tells us to give you ampicillin. Those are good drugs, and that's to make you get better. But there's something in the world called bad drugs, and people take them for all kinds of reasons, Cody, that you'll understand a little better when you get older."

And he looked at me and said, "Mommy, bad drugs are stupid."

I just thought, Oh, if only he feels this way forever.

Later on, they had these tremendously close close-ups of Mick Jagger and Keith Richards. To a small child, this can be a frightening sight. To me it can be a frightening sight. But Cody looked up into their faces and asked, "Mommy, why are their faces so horrible?"

I said, "Well, Cody, they've had rough lives."

Then he said something so interesting: "Do they have bad hearts?"

And I replied, "Cody, I don't know them; I don't know if they have bad hearts. I'm sure that they've done some bad things in their lives. But I don't know if they have bad hearts." Then we went to bed. I got my bath while Cody was waiting for me, and I came in and said, "Cody, ready to say prayers?"

He answered, "I already said them, Mom."

I couldn't believe it. I said, "Really?"

He said, "Yeah. And I prayed for those guys with the horrible faces to have good hearts."

Out of the mouths of babes. ❧

Every time I see Cody or pick up Cassidy, hold her tenderly, kiss her, or just wrestle with her—anything that's sweet—it reminds me so much of the way I felt about Michie, my baby sister, when she was little. And, to an extent, how I still feel about her today.

I'm more convinced than ever that if you make a child feel somehow included in the birth of the next child, they will take it very seriously. That child becomes theirs. I know it's only a few years into this, but Cody and Cassidy couldn't adore each other more. However, I think it's time for them to start taking baths separately. They're a little too fascinated with each other's plumbing. ⌒❧

Christmas was fast approaching, and as I do every year, I took stock of the year before, my hopes for the following year, and my attitude toward the season. I've always loved Christmas, but as the years go by, I've watched it become more and more commercial and less and less spiritual and meaningful in people's lives.

As a parent, I truly want Cody and Cassidy to focus on the manger in Bethlehem, and not on what's beneath the Christmas tree. The truth is, in terms of gifts, every day is Christmas for my children. I know it's unfair when you look at the plights of other children around the world, but Cody and Cassidy are blessed beyond belief. They even get gifts from strangers, every day of their lives. Many times those gifts are passed on to less fortunate children, but it's like anything else—after a while, if you get more than one thing, you become bored with it.

Cody and I have had lots of talks about what Christmas is all about. It's gift-giving time, but it's also God's gift to us as people, to show us how to live our lives, to make our lives meaningful, and to give our lives purpose. Even though he's only four-and-a-half this Christmas, he understands very well. I asked him the other day, "Cody, Christmas is . . . ?"

And he said, "It's not about what you get, it's what you give."

I said, "That's exactly right, honey." I was thrilled that he understood that. That doesn't mean he doesn't go lunging for everything he sees, but at least he has a basic concept that I hope will stay with him for the rest of his life. ❧

Christmas is coming, and Santa Claus is making appearances in a lot of the malls in our area. I want Cody to have the normal Christmas traditions that I'd had as a child, so I said, "Cody, let's go see Santa Claus."

He said, "Mommy, we have to see him at Stamford Mall."

I said, "Why Stamford Mall?"

He said, "That's where the *real* Santa is. The other guys are fakes."

So I said, "Oh, okay," and I take him to Stamford Mall. The line is incredibly long; it's going to be about an hour's wait to get to Santa's

lap. So we get in line, and Cody is incredibly chatty the entire hour, driving me crazy. Until we get to Santa. Then, of course, he clams up and he doesn't say a word. But he does sit on Santa's lap and gets his picture taken. Then we get in another line for the thrill of paying for this experience.

Finally we get up to where the lady is taking the money, and I look at her and say, "You know, Santa looks pretty beat. Santa looks like he has just about had it."

At which she looks at me and says, "Santa is *just fine*, thank you. Santa is my husband!"

Oh, boy, here we go. Deck the halls! ❧

We're in the midst of the Christmas season right now. I've kept gifts to a minimum; I've sent cards to all our friends who are as equally blessed as we are, saying that in lieu of giving gifts this year, we're going to make a donation to the Association to Benefit Children, in the hopes that other children's lives can be bettered, and in some cases, saved.

I think that more and more people are feeling this way as the years go by. The excesses are so obvious, and the needs are so obvious, that I think people feel less and less comfortable with amassing things in their lives. I know I'm not the least bit interested in that. I've given Frank only a couple of practical gifts. We feel good about making a difference in the world, even if it's just a little tiny corner of the world. Knowing that your life on this earth has in some way bettered someone else's life is a wonderful way to end the year. ❧

The other day we went to the premiere of *The Jungle Book*. I'm always thrilled to take Cody to the Disney movie premieres. It's one of the great perks of my job, since I work for Disney, that we get invited to these wonderful events. Cody brings his friends, and we have such a good time.

On this afternoon, I had to tape the David Letterman show and I got out late, so I got to the movie a little bit late. I've missed the first part, but now Mowgli is a young man. I settled down for the movie not knowing what to expect, except that I'd come to respect the Disney name, and you know you're going to get a good show. But I really wasn't sure if there was going to be any content in it that Cody wouldn't be quite ready for. (Though I guess after a year of Power Rangers, he'd be just about ready for anything.)

Some of the movie was pretty violent in terms of the animals, jungle life, and that sort of thing. I've got both guys on either side of me: Frank, who's sixty-four, and Cody, who's four.

Frank is entirely immersed in this movie—he loves it, but even Frank has a little adrenaline pumping there during some of the scenes. I look over at Cody to see if he's okay. He's just popping the popcorn into his mouth, and I say, "Codes, are you okay?"

He says, "I'm fine, Mommy, shhh!"

This kid is such a movie maven. He's going to grow up to be either Roger Ebert or Gene Siskel! I've never seen anything like it since I was a kid. Anyway, he absolutely fell in love with the movie. We all adored it; it was fabulous. I look over at Cody and he says, "It's party time!" I'm thinking, Oh, my gosh.

We go outside, and there are about forty paparazzi waiting to get a glimpse of anybody they could sell a picture of. They start snapping away when they see me, Cody, and Frank. Frank finally said, "Listen, guys, just take your picture; we'll give you a picture, and then leave us alone." Good old practical Frank.

So they start snapping away, and all of a sudden Cody steps out in front of the group and puts his arms out like a standup comedian and says, "Hasn't anybody told you guys I don't like pictures!"

I thought, Cody, I need to take some lessons from you about how to deal with the press. He totally disarmed them. They fell in love with him and it was just the cutest thing.

Later that night we went home, and Cody woke me up at four o'clock that morning to ask me a simple question. Some mothers get awakened with "Mommy, can I go pee-pee" or "Mommy, I need a glass of water." But Cody wakes me up and says, "Mommy, what is dinosaur DNA?"

That's what I get for letting him watch *Jurassic Park*.

The next morning, he comes in

about five in the morning and says, "Mommy, I've been coughing a lot."

I said, "Well, what would you like me to do about that?"

He said, "I think you should give me some cough medicine."

So I get him some cough medicine, and he says, "You know, what I think would really help my cough is if I get in bed with you and Daddy."

This kid's becoming Monty Hall. Everything's Let's Make A Deal. So I get him into bed, and of course once your kid's in bed with you, you can't help but love on them and cozy up to them and snuggle up to them. There's nothing sweeter than a kid in his pajamas. So he's lying there between me and Frank, and he's good for a little while. Finally he says, "Excuse me, but could somebody please give me a little room?" At least he was polite. 🍂

have no idea as the year ends what the new year holds. Nobody can know. When somebody asked me recently, "What do you want for the new year?" I replied as honestly as I possibly could. I said, "I just want more time to appreciate the things that I already have." That's the truth.

The authors' proceeds from this book will go to
The Cody Foundation for Cassidy's Place,
a home for HIV-positive and crack-addicted children.

About the Authors

Kathie Lee and Cody Gifford live with Frank and Cassidy Gifford in Connecticut. Kathie Lee appears every morning on *Live with Regis & Kathie Lee*. She is author of her bestselling autobiography, *I Can't Believe I said That!*, and coauthor with Regis Philbin of *Cooking with Regis & Kathie Lee* and *Entertaining with Regis & Kathie Lee.*

ABOUT THE ILLUSTRATOR

Kathie Lee Gifford fell in love with Sandra Forrest's children's book, *Fanny McFancy*, and asked her to do the illustrations for *Listen to My Heart*. Sandra Forrest has illustrated more than thirty books, including *Since Lulu Learned the Cancan, Wacky Wearables*, and *Baby Let's Eat*. She has also designed books for The Muppets, including *My First Muppet Dictionary*. Former design director of Welsh Publishing Group, Forrest is now an art director at Joshua Morris Publishing. She lives in Brooklyn, New York, and Ridgefield, Connecticut.